ROBERT INDIANA

RECENTPAINTINGS

PAUL KASMIN GALLERY 293 TENTH AVENUE, NEW YORK, NEW YORK 10001

© 2003

PAUL KASMIN GALLERY

New York, NY 10001

T: 212 563 4474

F: 212 563 4494

All Rights Reserved

ISBN 0-9713259-5-2

DESIGN:

Leslie Pirtle

PRODUCTION ASSOCIATE:

Allison Martone

PRODUCTION COORDINATION:

Anne Hamro

COLOR SEPARATION:

A. G. Martinetto

PRINTED IN ITALY BY:

Grafiche Ferrero

PHOTO CREDITS

COVER:

Dennis and Diana Griggs

ESSAY BY NATHAN KERNAN

THE FINALE OF
AN AMERICAN DREAM
ROBERT INDIANA'S NEW PAINTINGS

ROBERT INDIANA'S PAINTINGS ARE BOTH signs and *de*signs — that is, formalist abstractions —and also reconcile other seemingly opposite conditions or impulses: stasis and motion; revelation and concealment; memory and what is yet to come. As signs they encode references to Indiana's personal and our collective history, while as abstractions their appeal is to the senses, with contrasting and complementary colors that flicker and delight, and forms that satisfy the eye's hunger for balance and movement.

Robert Indiana's new paintings look like his old paintings — the quintessential Pop Art works with which he achieved international fame in the early sixties — except when they don't. That said, it is important to add that Indiana's new paintings are in no sense repetitions of earlier ones, but rather the seamless continuation of a project begun with his first major Pop art paintings, notably *The American Dream #1* of 1960-61. That painting has over the years engendered a series of American Dream paintings, accumulating meanings over the years, and culminating in the newest and final *Ninth American Dream* of 2001, and even more recent auxiliary works.

SIGNS OF A LIFE

Indiana's imagery and themes are deeply embedded in his personal history. Robert Clark, as he was then known, was born on September 13, 1928 in New Castle, Indiana. His parents, Earl and Carmen Clark, were hit by the Depression, and moved continually from one house to another, so that by the time he was seventeen Robert had lived in no fewer than twenty-one houses, mainly in Indianapolis. These houses were referred to in the family by their numerical order, which fascinated the boy. Automobiles were an important part of both his parents' lives, and Robert's father worked much of his life for the Phillips 66 company, whose bright red and green gas-station signs, bearing the numeral "66", were a prominent feature of the Midwest landscape, and an ever-present emblem of his father for young Robert. When Robert was ten, Earl Clark deserted the family and Carmen supported herself and her son as a cook in cafés. Robert's artistic aspirations were formed early, and he was "drawing and making pictures" since the age of six. After highschool, and a three year stint in the Air Force, he enrolled in the School of the Art Institute of Chicago on the GI Bill, graduating with a traveling fellowship in 1953. He chose to go to the University of Edinburgh, Scotland, where he studied botany, among other subjects, and developed an interest in writing poetry, setting it in metal type and printing it by hand at the Edinburgh College of Art.

The American Dream # 1, 1961
oil on canvas, 72 x 60 1/8 inches

In late 1954 Clark sailed for New York where he got a job in an art supply store on West 57th Street. There he met the almost equally young Ellsworth Kelly, who told him of a loft available near his own, downtown on Coenties Slip. Up to this point Clark's work was figurative, with something of a religious bent. Abstract-expressionism, then in full flower, was not of interest to him, but under the influence of Kelly and other artists on the Slip, such as Jack Youngerman and Agnes Martin, Clark developed a hard-edged biomorphic abstraction, producing in 1958 the extraordinary mural-sized *Stavrosis*, drybrushed in ink on 44 separate sheets of salvaged paper. *Stavrosis* is the Greek word for "Crucifixion" and the painting is an abstract "crucifixion" centered around a group of circles symbolizing Christ and the Apostles. Other forms in the work were derived from his study of botany, including what he calls the "avocado seed" shape and an early version of the double ginkgo leaf motif he continues to explore. It was at this time of renewed artistic identity that Robert Clark changed his name to Robert Indiana.

Continuing, by economic necessity, to use found materials, Indiana made a group of paintings of rows of monochrome circles on 4 x 8 foot plywood panels in 1959-60, and around the same time began a series - still continuing - of painted upright sculptures, "Herms", using wooden beams and columns found in and around his downtown studio. Much of the imagery used on the Herms, including circles, stars, stenciled numbers and words, was carried over onto canvas in Indiana's first mature Pop paintings, such as *American Dream #1*, of 1960-61, in which words were combined with rhythmically repeating geometric shapes. *American Dream #1* was acquired by the Museum of Modern Art in 1961, and in 1962 Indiana had his first solo show at the Stable Gallery. By the early 60's Indiana was regularly grouped with Warhol, Lichtenstein, Johns, Oldenburg, Rosenquist and others as one of the most important of what were being called "new realists" or Pop artists.

In 1969 on his first brief visit to Vinalhaven in Maine's Penobscot Bay, Indiana found one of the largest buildings on the island, the former Star of Hope Odd Fellow's Lodge, a magnificent nineteenth century mansard-roofed structure. It became his summer home until 1978, when, after 14 years on the Bowery occupying five floors of a former factory, he moved to the island full time. Indiana also has another studio in a nearby former sail loft. The interior of the Lodge, where he lives and works, has become a kind of *Gesamtkunstwerk*, presided over by the symbol of three interlocked ovals signifying "Friendship, Love and Truth", and filled with his paintings, prints, sculptures and extensive archives. Indiana, as he says, is a "keeper".

Unlike the Abstract-expressionists, the Pop artists arrived at their very different styles independently of each other, but even within this heterogeneous group, Indiana was something of an anomaly.

He was the only one — except for Ruscha in California a bit later — for whom words were important as subject matter, for one thing; and, even more radically within the context of late 20th century art, his work was not ironic. Indiana, as the late Gene Swenson was the first to observe, is a "sign painter", (he painted his first sign for his mother's doughnut shop when on leave from the Air Force) and his paintings are not dependent on the fine art or gallery environment — the rarefied "white cube" and the set of assumptions and references that comes with it — for their power or interest. As signs his paintings, not least the famous *Love* of 1966, speak a nearly universal language, such that, if the frames of reference of post-modern art were to vanish they would still evoke a response — would survive, like the ginkgo.

BOOK OF NUMBERS

Numbers, quantities and sequences, hold mysterious meanings. Etymologically, the English word "tell" is related to the German "zählen", to count, a sense that survives in certain usages, such as bank "teller". In Robert Indiana's paintings (and sculptures) numbers are used to "tell" narratives, or half-tell them, or recall them. Robert Indiana is often willing to tell us what specific words and numbers in his paintings mean to him, and it is an enrichment to know this. Such knowledge is also dangerous, however, and can give us a false sense of thinking we know what the painting *is*, when all it tells us is what it is "about", which in a sense, is exactly what it *is not*. The emblazoned sign can also be a mask, or like the diagonal "hazard" bars Indiana sometimes paints, a warding-off. As the poet James Schuyler said of the names of roses, "After learning all their names. . . it is important to forget them." In the same way, after learning the origins and meanings of Robert Indiana's private system of numerology, it is important — not to forget them, but to absorb them and let them nourish our own original and complete response to the painting. The paintings are bigger than the sum of their parts, and their meanings are not limited to those that Robert Indiana puts into them, but change as soon as the painting has been made, the way copper slowly oxidizes on exposure to air. Occasionally, they magically appear to grow into meanings that could not have been there when they were painted.

Of course, the materials of Indiana's "signs" — the words, letters, numbers and symbols that are the ostensible subjects of his paintings — are themselves "abstractions", yet when Indiana paints these "abstractions" as objects, they become in a real sense "concrete". Or hover in an ambiguous state between "abstraction" and "concreteness": here is "Love": we can look at it, touch it, hold it in our hands, sit on top of it, turn it upside down; here is the numeral "8": a quantity, a date, a month, perhaps, but also a specific form, bulbous, doubled, hollow-centered, infinitely re-turning into itself. Not enough has been said, perhaps, about Indiana's color — color that creates light with its contrasting, saturated hues set off by blacks, which never seem to be merely black. Or how this living, flickering, trembling light, in conjunction with precarious symmetry or partial symmetry, creates movement within stasis and suggests metamorphosis...

The Demuth American Dream # 5, 1963
oil on canvas, 144 x 144 inches

DREAM LIFE

At the heart of Robert Indiana's work of the past four decades has been his ongoing series of "American Dream" paintings. Retrospectively, *The First American Dream* can be seen as a kind of overture, introducing many of the themes and images that will reappear in later paintings: numbers, stars, words, circles, polygons, and diagonal "hazard" bars, etc.

With his two recent *Eighth American Dream* (2000) and *Ninth American Dream* (2001), Indiana completes the sequence. *The Eighth Dream* and its auxiliary painting, *October is in the Wind* (2000) relate to Indiana's mother, Carmen Watters Clark, who was born in Elizabethtown, Indiana, in August, the eighth month, and died, also in August, in Columbus, Indiana. Indiana arrived home to see her just before she died, and her last word to him was: "Eat". ("Eight" is a homophone for the past tense of "eat".) The texts used in the *Eighth American Dream*, "August is Memory" and "August is bittersweet" come from a poem Indiana / Clark wrote in his mother's memory in 1953, while the lines "October / is in the wind" on the painting of that title are the opening of a poem written by Indiana (as Robert Clark) in 1945. In that painting the numeral "8" refers to the month of October, the eighth month in the Roman calendar, while its bosomy shape may also suggest maternity.

Turn, Turn, Turn.

The magnificent *Ninth American Dream* (2001) is a kind of retrospective of Indiana's life, as well as a summary of many previously expressed texts and themes. Former and present homes are named: "Coenties Slip", "The Bowery", "Penobscot Bay": as Indiana has said, "All of my memories are very much connected to geography." A sense of movement pervades the work, from its precarious balance as a square upended to form a regular diamond, to the rotating orientations of the "hazard" stripes behind the manifestations of the numeral "9" around the perimeter, to its flickering contrasting hues. Auxiliary paintings to the *Ninth Dream,* such as *Nonending Nonagon* (2001) and *Remember November* (2000) center the numeral 9 within nonagons — of the polygons he has painted, the nonagon is the one that most closely approaches a circle, just as the number nine anticipates zero, or 10 (in the past he continued his Cardinal Numbers series to eleven and twelve but has since decided to limit them to 1 through 0) and zero, of course, is a circle, the circle that drives his work, from the parental automobile wanderlust, to "nonending" circular texts, such as

"Love is God", derived from the reversal of a Sunday school motto of Indiana's childhood. *Remember November* is an extraordinarily haunting and prescient image, conjoining as it does the number 9 with the 11th month, though it, along with *Terror in November* (2000), were painted well before September 11, 2001, in protest against the "hijacking" of the November, 2000 presidential election in Florida. The association of November with the *Ninth Dream* comes through the Latin origin of the word November, originally the ninth month in the Roman Calendar.

The 6666 American Dream (2002), and auxiliary paintings, *US 66 (Cities)* and *US 66 (States)* (both 2002) refer to *The Sixth Dream USA 666*, which was completed in 1966, just after Indiana learned of his father's death in June (the sixth month). Earl Clark not only worked for Phillips 66, he also disappeared from Robert and Carmen's lives on Route 66. However, in the sense that 6 is also the reverse of 9, *The 6666 American Dream* should also perhaps be understood as an auxiliary to the *Ninth American Dream* of the previous year. In *The 6666 American Dream* the actual of the numerals 6 and 9 is seen to be identical, the 6 within the top quadrant revolving around the center of the composition to become the 9 of the bottom quadrant, and back to 6 again at the top, moving through "sideways" 9's or 6's in the left and right hand quadrants. Here the meaning of a shape changes with, is inherent in, its orientation — or "orientation": 9 is a queer 6, and *The Ninth Dream*, which is partly a self-portrait, is also an "inversion" of the paternal *Sixth Dream*.

Ginkgo

The ginkgo is sacred in China, and in New York a common street tree, whose bright yellow fan-shaped leaves pave our fall streets with gold. It is the Alpha and Omega of the plant world: among the oldest plants surviving from pre-historic times, the similarity of its present-day form to fossilized remains led Darwin to dub it a "living fossil" while at the other end of the timeline, two ginkgo trees are known to have survived the atomic blast at Hiroshima, one in a temple about a kilometer from the blast center. In Robert Indiana's *Ginkgo* painting (2000) two stylized ginkgo leaves are depicted stem to

The Seventh American Dream, 1998
oil on canvas,
204 x 204
inches
4 panels,
72 x 72
inches, each

stem make a loose numeral "8". The painting is of course a deliberate reprise of, though quite different from, his earlier *Gingko*, painted in 1959, a seminal work (in more ways than one), formally poised between his botanically-inspired *Stavrosis* of a year earlier, with its more testicular ginkgo leaf motive, and his "orb" paintings of about 1959 also. The new *Ginkgo* is spelled differently to allow a play on the word "go", which is incorporated into the surrounding text, "Go from Coenties Slip thence to Vinalhaven". The text summarizes Indiana's history in terms of "going" from one home to another, but being in the imperative mood, rather than the past tense, it reads more like a prophecy than history. The word "Go" might be Indiana's mantra, encompassing a circular "O", which is also a wheel, and an ever-turning cycle of creativity. In the arena of his paintings time does stand still, or rather is circular, and constantly renewed.

CATALOGUE

1

The X-7, 1998

Oil on canvas

170 x 170 inches assembled

5 panels

2

The Ninth Love Cross, 2001

Oil on canvas

108 x 108 inches, cross shape

5 panels

3

The Ninth American Dream, 2001

Oil on canvas

153 x 153 inches, diamond

9 panels

4

The Eighth American Dream, 2000

Oil on canvas

170 x 170 inches, diamond

4 panels

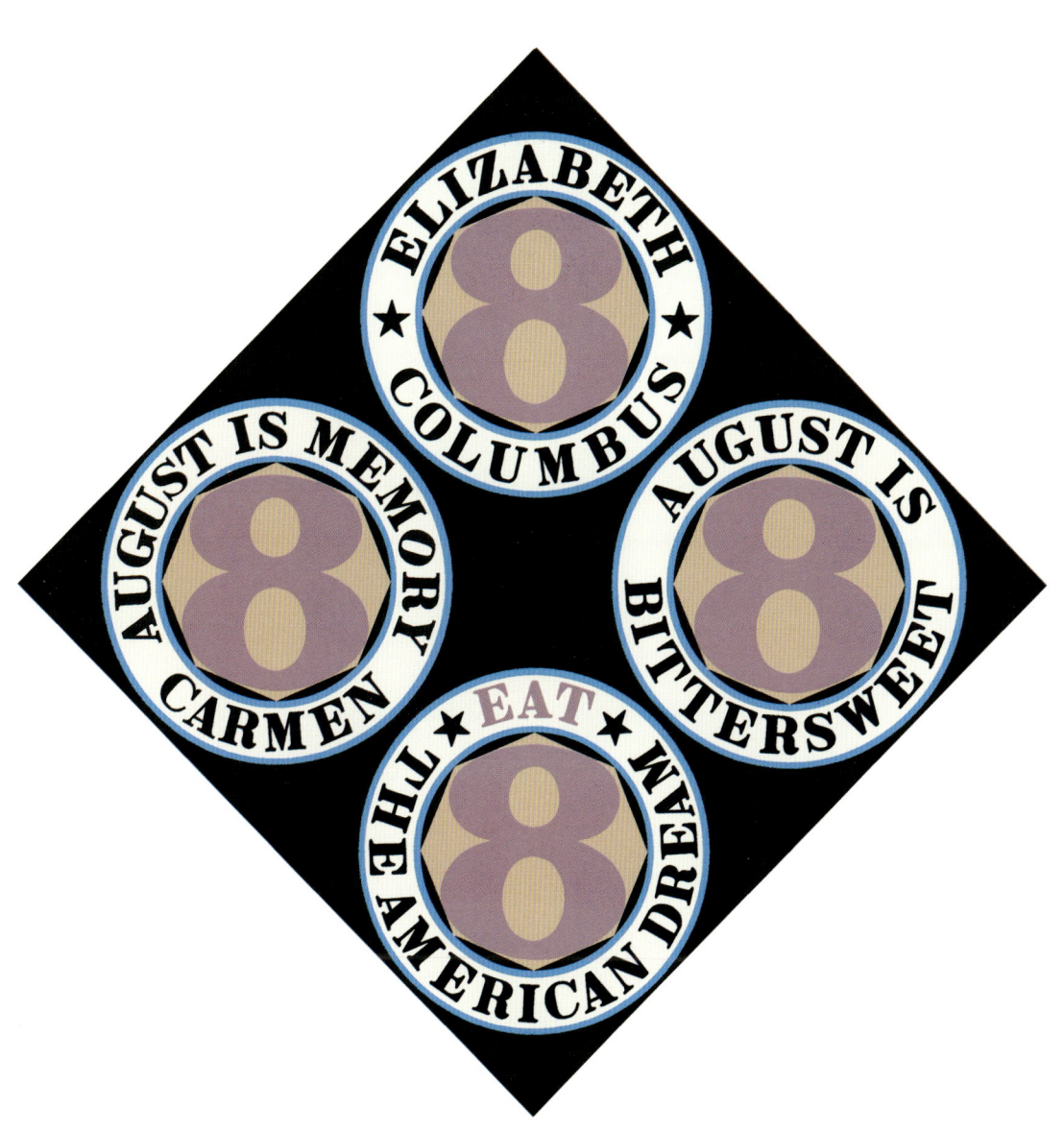

5
Ginkgo, 2000
Oil on canvas
60 x 50 inches

6

Terror in November, 2000

Oil on canvas

68 x 68 inches, diamond

7

October is in the Wind, 2000

Oil on canvas

60 x 60 inches

8

Remember November, 2000

Oil on canvas

60 x 60 inches

9
Nonending Nonagon, 2001
Oil on canvas
70 x 60 inches

10

Nocturnal Nonagon, 2001

Oil on canvas

70 x 60 inches

NONAGON

11

The 6666, The American Dream, 2002

Oil on canvas

136 x 136 inches, diamond

4 panels

LOVE IN LOVE IN LOVE
66
TO THE MOON
69
TO VINALHAVEN
69
THE AMERICAN DREAM
60

12
US 66, (States), 2002
Oil on canvas
101.5 x 101.5 inches, diamond
diptych1 of 2

ILLINOIS
U
6
S
MISSOURI
KANSAS
6
OKLAHOMA
TEXAS
6
NEW MEXICO
ARIZONA
6
CALIFORNIA

13
US 66, (Cities), 2002
Oil on canvas
101.5 x 101.5 inches, diamond
diptych 2 of 2

CHICAGO
6
ST. LOUIS
GALENA
TULSA
AMARILLO
ALBUQUERQUE
FLAGSTAFF
9
LOS ANGELES

CATALOGUE CHECKLIST

1

The X-7, 1998
Oil on canvas
170 x 170 inches assembled
5 panels
Photo credit: Dennis and Diana Griggs
Copyright Robert Indiana
Artists Rights Society (ARS), New York

2

The Ninth Love Cross, 2001
Oil on canvas
108 x 108 inches, cross shape
5 panels
Photo credit: Adam Reich
Copyright Robert Indiana
Artists Rights Society (ARS), New York

3

The Ninth American Dream, 2001
Oil on canvas
153 x 153 inches, diamond
9 panels
Photo credit: Dennis and Diana Griggs
Copyright Robert Indiana
Artists Rights Society (ARS), New York

4

The Eighth American Dream, 2000
Oil on canvas
170 x 170 inches, diamond
4 panels
Photo credit: Adam Reich
Copyright Robert Indiana
Artists Rights Society (ARS), New York

5

Ginkgo, 2000
Oil on canvas
60 x 50 inches
Photo credit: Dennis and Diana Griggs
Copyright Robert Indiana
Artists Rights Society (ARS), New York

6

Terror in November, 2000
Oil on canvas
68 x 68 inches, diamond
Photo credit: Dennis and Diana Griggs
Copyright Robert Indiana
Artists Rights Society (ARS), New York

7

October is in the Wind, 2000
Oil on canvas
60 x 60 inches
Photo credit: Dennis and Diana Griggs
Copyright Robert Indiana
Artists Rights Society (ARS), New York

8

Remember November, 2000
Oil on canvas
60 x 60 inches
Photo credit: Dennis and Diana Griggs
Copyright Robert Indiana
Artists Rights Society (ARS), New York

9

Nonending Nonagon, 2001
Oil on canvas
70 x 60 inches
Photo credit: Dennis and Diana Griggs
Copyright Robert Indiana
Artists Rights Society (ARS), New York

10

Nocturnal Nonagon, 2001
Oil on canvas
70 x 60 inches
Photo credit: Dennis and Diana Griggs
Copyright Robert Indiana
Artists Rights Society (ARS), New York

11

The 6666, The American Dream, 2002
Oil on canvas
136 x 136 inches, diamond
4 panels
Photo credit: Camerarts
Copyright Robert Indiana
Artists Rights Society (ARS), New York

12

US 66, (States), 2002
Oil on canvas
101.5 x 101.5 inches, diamond
diptych 1 of 2
Photo credit: Dennis and Diana Griggs
Copyright Robert Indiana
Artists Rights Society (ARS), New York

13

US 66, (Cities), 2002
Oil on canvas
101.5 x 101.5 inches, diamond
diptych 2 of 2
Photo credit: Dennis and Diana Griggs
Copyright Robert Indiana
Artists Rights Society (ARS), New York

ESSAY CREDITS

PAGE 7
The Star of Hope, Vinalhaven
October 2001
©Morgan Art Foundation, Ltd.
Artist Rights Society (ARS), New York

PAGE 8
The American Dream #!, 1961
Oil on canvas
72 x 60 1/8 inches
The Museum of Modern Art, New York
Larry Aldrich Foundation Fund

PAGE 10
The Demuth American Dream #5, 1963
Oil on canvas
144 x 144 inches
Art Gallery of Toronto
Gift from the Women's Committee Fund, 1964
©2002 Morgan Art Foundation, Ltd.
Artists Rights Society (ARS), New York

PAGE 10
The Seventh American Dream, 1998
Oil on canvas
204 x 204 inches
4 panels, each 72 x 72 inches
Courtesy Collection Fonds National d'Art Contemporain
©2002 Morgan Art Foundation, Ltd.
Artists Rights Society (ARS), New York